MATHWORKS!

Using Math to **Win a GRAND PRIX**

zepter cosmetics

vodafone

HSBC

GARETH STEVENS
GS
PUBLISHING
A World Almanac Education Group Company

by
Wendy and David Clemson
and Jonathan Noble

Please visit our web site at: www.garethstevens.com
For a free color catalog describing Gareth Stevens Publishing's
list of high-quality books and multimedia programs, call
1-800-542-2595 (USA) or 1-800-387-3178 (Canada).
Gareth Stevens Publishing's fax: (414) 332-3567.

Library of Congress Cataloging-in-Publication Data

Clemson, Wendy.
    Using math to win a Grand Prix / by Wendy and David
Clemson and Jonathan Noble. — North American ed.
        p. cm. — (Mathworks!)
    ISBN 0-8368-4214-6 (lib. bdg.)
    1. Mathematics—Problems, exercises, etc.—Juvenile
literature. 2. Grand Prix racing—Juvenile literature.
I. Clemson, David. II. Noble, Jonathan. III. Title.
IV. Series.
QA43.C66   2004
510'.76—dc22   2004045324

This North American edition first published in 2005 by
Gareth Stevens Publishing
A World Almanac Education Group Company
330 West Olive Street, Suite 100
Milwaukee, Wisconsin 53212

The publishers thank the following consultants for their kind
assistance: Jenni Back and Liz Pumfrey (NRICH Project,
Cambridge University) and Debra Voege.

Gareth Stevens Editor: Jim Mezzanotte
Gareth Stevens Art Direction: Tammy West

Photo credits (t=top, b=bottom, c=center, l=left, r=right)
Alamy: front cover, 20 (bc). Redzone Motorsport Images
(John Marsh): back cover, 1, 11 (c), 12-13, 15, 18-19, 20 (tr),
21 (cl, bl), 26-27 (c). Sporting Pictures: 2-3, 9, 11 (t, b),
16-17, 20 (br), 20 (bl), 23, 24-25, 27 (cr).

Printed in the United States of America

1 2 3 4 5 6 7 8 9 08 07 06 05 04

CONTENTS

HAVE FUN WITH MATH

How to Use This Book

Math is important in the daily lives of people everywhere. We use math when we play games, ride bicycles, or go shopping, and everyone uses math at work. Imagine you are a top Formula One racing driver. You may not realize it, but a Formula One driver uses math to help plan a strategy for winning a race. In this book, you will be able to try lots of exciting math activities as you learn what it is like to drive in a Formula One Grand Prix. If you can work with numbers, shapes, measurements, charts, and diagrams, then you can WIN A GRAND PRIX.

How does it feel to drive a race car?

Take the wheel and find out how it feels to go 200 miles per hour in a Formula One race.

Math Activities

The driver's clipboards have math activities for you to try. Get your pencil, ruler, and notebook (for figuring out problems and listing answers).

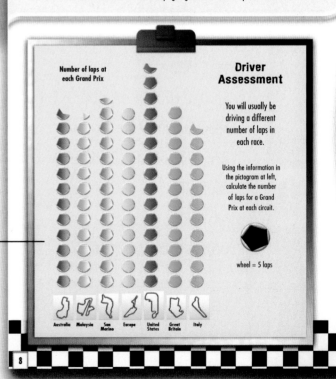

THE GRAND PRIX CIRCUITS

Grand Prix circuits, or race tracks, have straights and many kinds of turns, from sweeping curves to tight hairpins. Every circuit is different. One trip around a circuit is called a lap. Except for the race at Monaco, a Grand Prix is always run to the least number of complete laps over 305 kilometers (km). The number of laps varies from circuit to circuit. The Belgium Grand Prix at Spa-Francorchamps, for example, is only 44 laps, because a single lap at that circuit is very long. At other Grand Prix circuits, races are over 70 laps, because the laps at those circuits are much shorter. Get to know the Grand Prix circuits by figuring out the number of laps for each race.

Number of laps at each Grand Prix

Driver Assessment

You will usually be driving a different number of laps in each race.

Using the information in the pictogram at left, calculate the number of laps for a Grand Prix at each circuit.

wheel = 5 laps

Australia   Malaysia   San Marino   Europe   United States   Great Britain   Italy

8

NEED HELP?

- **If you are not sure how to do some of the math problems, turn to pages 28 and 29, where you will find lots of tips to help get you started.**

- **Turn to pages 30 and 31 to check your answers.**
(Try all the activities and challenges before you look at the answers.)

- **Turn to page 32 for definitions of some words and terms used in the book.**

Circuit Fact

The Spa-Francorchamps circuit in Belgium is the longest Grand Prix circuit. The length of a lap is 6.97 kilometers. The Belgium Grand Prix lasts for 44 laps, which is a total distance of 306.68 kilometers.

Circuit Fact

Monaco has the shortest Grand Prix circuit, with a lap that measures 3.34 kilometers. The total length of the Monaco Grand Prix is 260.52 kilometers. The drivers have to race around the track 78 times!

DATA BOX

Grand Prix Circuits

GRAND PRIX	LAP LENGTH	NUMBER OF LAPS PER GRAND PRIX
AUSTRALIA	5.3 km	?
MALAYSIA	5.5 km	?
BAHRAIN	5.4 km	57
SAN MARINO	4.9 km	?
SPAIN	4.6 km	66
MONACO	3.3 km	78
EUROPE	5.1 km	?
CANADA	4.4 km	70
UNITED STATES	4.2 km	?
FRANCE	4.4 km	70
GREAT BRITAIN	5.1 km	?
GERMANY	4.6 km	67
HUNGARY	4.4 km	70
BELGIUM	7.0 km	44
ITALY	5.8 km	?
CHINA	5.5 km	56
JAPAN	5.8 km	53
BRAZIL	4.3 km	71

Some of the circuits in this data box are missing their lap numbers. You can calculate how many laps these circuits have by using the pictogram in the Driver's Assessment on page 8.

Math Facts and Data

To complete some of the math activities, you will need information from a DATA BOX, which looks like this.

You will find lots of amazing details about Formula One race cars, drivers, and Grand Prix races in FACT boxes that look like this.

Math Challenge

The DATA BOX above shows the lap distances for each Grand Prix circuit. Use the information in the box to answer the following questions.

1) Which circuits have a lap length that is less than Australia but more than San Marino?
2) If the lap lengths were rounded to the nearest kilometer, which tracks would be 6 kilometers long?

Malaysian Grand Prix at Sepang

Math Challenge

Blue boxes, like this one, have extra math questions to challenge you. Give them a try!

9

The life of a race car driver can be very exciting. Top Formula One drivers get to travel all over the world. They fly first class or in their own jets, and they stay in the best hotels or in luxury apartments. They also get to meet many other celebrities! The drivers work hard, however, and they have busy schedules. On the weekend of a Grand Prix, they have a lot to do even when they are not in their cars. They have to go to meetings to discuss the best strategy to use during the race, and they also have to attend press conferences and parties hosted by their sponsors. A new Grand Prix season is about to begin. It is time for drivers to make their travel plans.

Driver Assessment

Formula One races are held in many different countries, so the drivers do a lot of traveling.

You are a top Formula One driver, and you live in Monaco. Using the information in the DATA BOX on page 7, calculate some distances that you will need to travel during the new Formula One Grand Prix season.

1) Not including the race in Monaco, what is the shortest and longest distance you will travel to get to a race?
2) What is the difference in travel distance between the trip to Canada and the trip to Great Britain?
3) How much farther is it to Malaysia than to Bahrain?
4) By how many miles is the trip to Brazil shorter than the trip to Japan?
5) If you go home to Monaco after each race, how far do you travel in August?

Race Fact

Each Formula One racing team takes over 30 tons of equipment to every race. This equipment includes 3 fully-built chassis, 17,000 spare parts, 10 engines, 5 gearboxes, 172 wheels, 5 steering wheels, and 6 helmets!

What Is Formula One?

Formula One is a set of rules for single-seater racing cars. The cars have to be built to a special set of design specifications, including safety measures to protect the drivers. A car built to these specifications is a Formula One car, and a race between these cars is a Formula One Grand Prix.

DATA BOX

The Formula One Season

DATE	GRAND PRIX (LOCATION)	MILES FROM MONACO
March 7	Australia (Melbourne)	10,193
March 21	Malaysia (Sepang)	6,298
April 4	Bahrain (Manama)	2,680
April 25	San Marino (Imola)	303
May 9	Spain (Barcelona)	424
May 23	Monaco (Monte Carlo)	0
May 30	Europe (Nürburgring)	560
June 13	Canada (Montreal)	3,833
June 20	United States (Indianapolis)	4,583
July 4	France (Magny-Cours)	454
July 11	Great Britain (Silverstone)	825
July 25	Germany (Hockenheim)	543
August 15	Hungary (Budapest)	612
August 29	Belgium (Spa-Francorchamps)	665
September 12	Italy (Monza)	199
September 26	China (Shanghai)	5,794
October 10	Japan (Suzuka)	6,128
October 24	Brazil (Sao Paolo)	5,772

Math Challenge

Here is a month in a driver's calendar.

Sunday	Monday	Tuesday	Wednesday	Thursday	Friday	Saturday
				1	2 PRACTICE	3 Qualifying
RACE DAY 4	5	6	7	8	9 PRACTICE	10 Qualifying
RACE DAY 11	12	13	14	15	16	17
18	19	20	21	22	23 PRACTICE	24 Qualifying
RACE DAY 25	26	27	28	29	30	31

Use the calendar above to answer these questions:

1) Which month is shown on the calendar?

2) Where is the driver racing on the second Sunday of the month?

THE GRAND PRIX CIRCUITS

Grand Prix circuits, or race tracks, have straights and many kinds of turns, from sweeping curves to tight hairpins. Every circuit is different. One trip around a circuit is called a lap. Except for the race at Monaco, a Grand Prix is always run to the least number of complete laps over 305 kilometers (km). The number of laps varies from circuit to circuit. The Belgium Grand Prix at Spa-Francorchamps, for example, is only 44 laps, because a single lap at that circuit is very long. At other Grand Prix circuits, races are over 70 laps, because the laps at those circuits are much shorter. Get to know the Grand Prix circuits by figuring out the number of laps for each race.

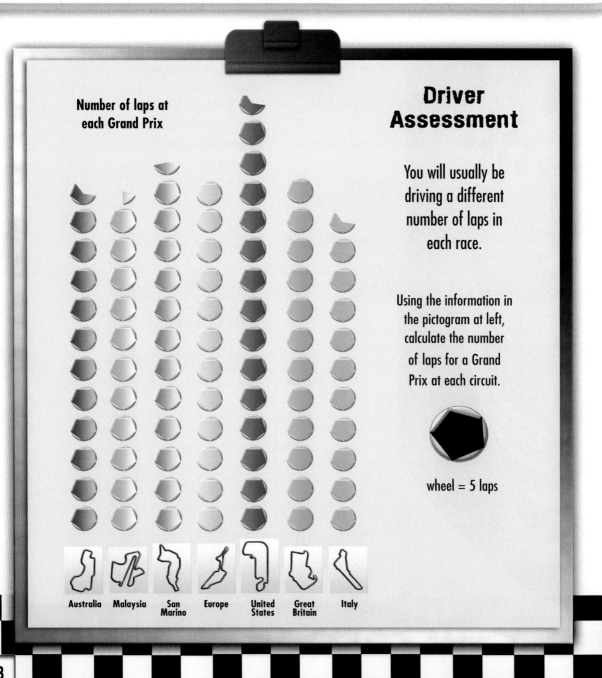

Number of laps at each Grand Prix

Driver Assessment

You will usually be driving a different number of laps in each race.

Using the information in the pictogram at left, calculate the number of laps for a Grand Prix at each circuit.

wheel = 5 laps

Australia   Malaysia   San Marino   Europe   United States   Great Britain   Italy

Circuit Fact

The Spa-Francorchamps circuit in Belgium is the longest Grand Prix circuit. The length of a lap is 6.97 kilometers. The Belgium Grand Prix lasts for 44 laps, which is a total distance of 306.68 kilometers.

Circuit Fact

Monaco has the shortest Grand Prix circuit, with a lap that measures 3.34 kilometers. The total length of the Monaco Grand Prix is 260.52 kilometers. The drivers have to race around the track 78 times!

DATA BOX

Grand Prix Circuits

GRAND PRIX	LAP LENGTH	NUMBER OF LAPS PER GRAND PRIX
AUSTRALIA	5.3 km	?
MALAYSIA	5.5 km	?
BAHRAIN	5.4 km	57
SAN MARINO	4.9 km	?
SPAIN	4.6 km	66
MONACO	3.3 km	78
EUROPE	5.1 km	?
CANADA	4.4 km	70
UNITED STATES	4.2 km	?
FRANCE	4.4 km	70
GREAT BRITAIN	5.1 km	?
GERMANY	4.6 km	67
HUNGARY	4.4 km	70
BELGIUM	7.0 km	44
ITALY	5.8 km	?
CHINA	5.5 km	56
JAPAN	5.8 km	53
BRAZIL	4.3 km	71

Some of the circuits in this data box are missing their lap numbers. You can calculate how many laps these circuits have by using the pictogram in the Driver's Assessment on page 8.

Malaysian Grand Prix at Sepang

Math Challenge

The DATA BOX above shows the lap distances for each Grand Prix circuit. Use the information in the box to answer the following questions.

1) Which circuits have a lap length that is less than Australia but more than San Marino?
2) If the lap lengths were rounded to the nearest kilometer, which tracks would be 6 kilometers long?

In order to drive in a Formula One Grand Prix, a racing driver must have a "super license." This special license is given to only drivers who have been successful in other, similar forms of auto racing or to drivers who have completed enough miles testing a Formula One car. Formula One racing is all about teamwork, however, and success depends on more than just qualified drivers. Racing teams, known as constructors, design and build the best Formula One cars possible. Then each team's drivers use their skills to win on the track. Every season, there are two titles up for grabs — the Drivers World Championship and the Constructors World Championship.

Driver Assessment

Driving a Formula One car takes a lot of strength and stamina. You need to be in excellent shape.

These stopwatches show your training times for last season and this season. Use them to answer the following questions.

1) In which activities have your times improved? By how many seconds have they improved?
2) In which activity has your time become slower? By how many seconds do you need to improve your time to match last season's time?

	Last season	This season
CYCLING 6 miles	14:10 minutes seconds	13:55 minutes seconds
RUNNING 1/2 mile	03:59 minutes seconds	03:38 minutes seconds
SWIMMING 5 lengths	02:56 minutes seconds	03:02 minutes seconds

Math Challenge

You keep a diary that lists your training activities for the Formula One season.

1) How many hours a week did you spend in the gym?
2) In total, how many hours did you spend training each week?

MONDAY	9 – 11 gym	4 – 5 swimming
TUESDAY	8 – 9 running	2 – 5:30 gym
WEDNESDAY	8 – 9 running 9 – 10:45 gym	3 – 6:15 swimming
THURSDAY	8 – 10 cycling	3:30 – 5:30 swimming
FRIDAY	9 – 11:20 gym	3 – 5:10 swimming

WILLIAMSF1

CONSTRUCTORS WORLD TITLES: 9

JUAN PABLO MONTOYA
DATE OF BIRTH: September 20, 1975
DEBUT: Australia 2001
FIRST WIN: Italy 2001

RALF SCHUMACHER
DATE OF BIRTH: June 30, 1975
DEBUT: Australia 1997
FIRST WIN: San Marino 2001

Ralf Schumacher inside his car

RENAULT

CONSTRUCTORS WORLD TITLES: 0

JARNO TRULLI
DATE OF BIRTH: July 13, 1974
DEBUT: Australia 1997

FERNANDO ALONSO
DATE OF BIRTH: July 29, 1981
DEBUT: Australia 2001
FIRST WIN: Hungary 2003

MCLAREN

CONSTRUCTORS WORLD TITLES: 8

DAVID COULTHARD
DATE OF BIRTH: March 27, 1971
DEBUT: Spain 1994
FIRST WIN: Portugal 1995

KIMI RAIKKONEN
DATE OF BIRTH: October 17, 1979
DEBUT: Australia 2001
FIRST WIN: Malaysia 2003

Montoya, Coulthard, and Raikkonen

BAR

CONSTRUCTORS WORLD TITLES: 0

JENSON BUTTON
DATE OF BIRTH: January 19, 1980
DEBUT: Australia 2000

TAKUMA SATO
DATE OF BIRTH: January 28, 1977
DEBUT: Australia 2002

FERRARI

CONSTRUCTORS WORLD TITLES: 13

MICHAEL SCHUMACHER
DATE OF BIRTH: January 3, 1969
DEBUT: Belgium 1991
FIRST WIN: Belgium 1992
DRIVERS' TITLES: 6

RUBENS BARRICHELLO
DATE OF BIRTH: May 23, 1972
DEBUT: South Africa 1993
FIRST WIN: Germany 2000

Michael Schumacher rides by his cheering Ferrari team.

Driver Fact

During a race, drivers need protection from accidents. They wear special overalls made from a material called Nomex that can resist fire for 12 seconds. Drivers also wear Nomex underwear, a fireproof cap and an ultra strong helmet, fireproof racing gloves, and racing boots that have rubber soles for maximum grip on the pedals.

IS YOUR CAR READY TO RACE?

Formula One teams have to follow very strict rules when constructing their cars. If a Formula One car breaks any of these rules, it will be disqualified! These rules specify the length, height, and weight of the car and the size of its tires. Certain safety features, such as roll bars, leak-resistant fuel tanks, and protection for the driver's head and neck, are also specified in the rules. A Formula One car is made up of 80,000 parts and contains more than a half mile of wiring. One car costs more than 1.5 million dollars!

Driver Assessment

Formula One cars are usually about the same size and weight.

Look at the photograph of a Formula One car at right. Then, estimate the size and weight of the car and choose from the following figures.

1) The width of the car is about:
   a) 25 inches   b) 6 feet   c) 4 feet

2) The length of the car is approximately:
   a) 12 feet   b) 25 feet   c) 8 feet

3) The car with driver weighs at least:
   a) 500 pounds
   b) 8,000 pounds
   c) 1,330 pounds

Technical Fact

Formula One rules state that the car with the driver has to weigh more than a certain amount. If the car is too light, ballast (a heavy material) such as metal is added to make up the weight. The fit in the car's cockpit is so tight that the driver can only get in and out of the car if the steering wheel is removed!

Tire Fact

The tires on a Formula One car are up to about 14 inches wide. Normal car tires are only about 7 inches wide. Formula One cars have different tires for wet weather and for dry weather.

Math Challenge

To build a Formula One car, one person would have to work nonstop for about 240,000 hours, or about 27 years!

1) If 10 people were building the car, how many hours would each person have to work?

2) If 100 people were building the car, how many hours would each person have to work?

In real life, a team of 300 people usually builds a Formula One car.

The team still needs 240,000 hours to build the car.

3) How many hours will each person in the team have to work?

4) If each person works for 10 hours a day, how many days will it take to build the car?

Michael Schumacher drives his Ferrari.

Technical Fact

Throughout a race weekend, special officials called scrutineers closely watch and check all the Formula One cars. The scrutineers make sure that racing teams do not break any rules while they are working on their cars and preparing them for the race.

Tire Fact

At top speed, the tires on a Formula One car rotate fifty times a second! The tires are designed to last up to 75 miles. The tires on normal cars are usually made to last up to 60,000 miles!

GET SET FOR THE MONACO GRAND PRIX

I t is the weekend of the exciting Monaco Grand Prix. In Monte Carlo, some of the city streets are closed down to make the circuit, and the drivers actually race on normal roads! The cars hurtle along past the harbor and past casinos and hotels. They zoom up hills, around bends, and even through a tunnel. Passing other cars is difficult on this circuit, and the team with the best strategy usually wins. Before the start of the race on Sunday, your team will need to make some important strategy decisions.

Driver Assessment

Before the race, your team has to decide on some adjustments to the car so it will go as fast as possible. The team has to set the angle of the car's wings for the right amount of downforce, so the car stays firmly on the road but is still fast. The team also has to decide which gear setting to use.

Downforce

You make three laps around the Monaco track. Your car has a low downforce setting for the first lap, a medium downforce setting for the second lap, and a high downforce setting for the third lap. The diagram of the Monaco circuit on page 15 shows the track split up into three sectors. Your team records how fast you go in each sector with each downforce setting.

	Sector 1 time in seconds	Sector 2 time in seconds	Sector 3 time in seconds
LOW setting	19.5	37.4	18.4
MEDIUM setting	19.3	37.2	18.2
HIGH setting	19.6	37.1	17.9

1) For each downforce setting, add the three sector times. Which setting gives the fastest lap time?

Gear Settings

You make three more laps around the track. Your car has a low gear setting for the first lap, a medium gear setting for the second lap, and a high gear setting for the third lap. Your team records how fast you go in each sector with each gear setting.

	Sector 1 time in seconds	Sector 2 time in seconds	Sector 3 time in seconds
LOW setting	19.4	37.1	17.9
MEDIUM setting	19.4	37.0	18.1
HIGH setting	19.5	37.1	18.2

2) For each gear setting, add the three sector times. Which gear setting gives the fastest lap time?

Car Fact

When a Grand Prix is run on a street course, manhole covers are welded down because the cars running over them can cause the covers to lift up.

Downforce

Formula One cars have wings that are like upside down airplane wings. An airplane's wings are designed to create lift, but a Formula One car's wings create an opposite effect called downforce. This effect pushes the car down, helping it stick to the track. The downforce that these wings create at 100 miles per hour could actually hold the car to the ceiling of a tunnel, so the car could drive upside down! So far, however, no one has tried this stunt.

Math Challenge

The downforce created by a Formula One car's wings depends on their angle to the ground. Less angle creates less downforce, and more angle creates more downforce. A car with less downforce also has less drag, or resistance to the air, so the car will go faster. A car with more downforce has more drag, so it will have more grip on the corners but will go slower on the straights.

Test your knowledge of angles. Which of the angles below is 90°, 60°, 30°, 180°, 45°?

1)

2)

3)

4)

5)

in the tunnel at Monaco

Monaco Circuit

Sector 1

Sector 3

Tunnel

Sector 2

A Formula One car has wings in front and in back.

15

PLANNING YOUR PIT STOPS

During a race, Formula One cars need to make pit stops. The drivers pull off the track into a special area called the pits. During a pit stop, a team's pit crew refuels the car, changes the tires, and checks to make sure the car is running properly. Formula One teams have to decide how many pit stops their cars will make in a race and how much fuel the cars will carry. If a car carries a lot of fuel, the weight of the fuel will slow the car down. If a car carries less fuel, however, it will have to make more pit stops, which will cost vital seconds. For every race, teams have to decide on the best strategy for carrying fuel and making pit stops.

Driver Assessment

Before the Monaco Grand Prix begins, your team will have to decide on the best strategy for pit stops. You can make one, two, or three pit stops during the race.

Use the DATA BOX on page 17 to answer the following questions.

Keep in mind that your car should be completely empty of fuel as it goes into the pits.

1) If you make 1 pit stop, how many liters of fuel will you need at the start of the race? Approximately how many gallons of fuel will you need?

2) If you make 2 pit stops, how many liters of fuel will you need at your first pit stop?

3) If you make 3 pit stops, how many liters of fuel will you need at each pit stop?

Fuel Fact

For every 3.5 gallons of fuel that a Formula One car carries, it loses 0.3 seconds of time per lap. As the fuel is used, the car can race around the track faster.

DATA BOX

Monaco Grand Prix Pit Stops

TOTAL NUMBER OF LAPS AT MONACO		78
AMOUNT OF FUEL USED PER LAP		4 liters
PIT STOP STRATEGY		
One pit stop during race	Stop on lap:	39
Two pit stops during race	Stop on laps:	26 and 52
Three pit stops during race	Stop on laps:	19 and 38 and 57

Math Challenge

For safety, most Grand Prix circuits have fences around their perimeters (boundaries).

1) A fence being built around a race circuit will enclose a rectangular area. The area is 7,385 feet long and 3,920 feet wide. What is the perimeter of the area?

2) What is your estimate of the perimeter of this rectangle?
   a) 8 inches
   b) 6 inches
   c) 2 inches

3) The perimeter of a regular hexagon is 30 inches. What is the length of each side?

WILL YOU MAKE POLE POSITION?

At the start of a Grand Prix, cars are arranged in a grid, which is two lines of cars with one line slightly ahead of the other line. The position of a car on the grid depends on how well the driver does in the qualifying session, which takes place the day before the race. For the qualifying session, each driver makes three laps on the circuit. During the middle lap, or "flying lap," the cars are timed. The cars are put in order based on the drivers' times. If you have the best time, you will get to be in the pole position, at the head of the grid!

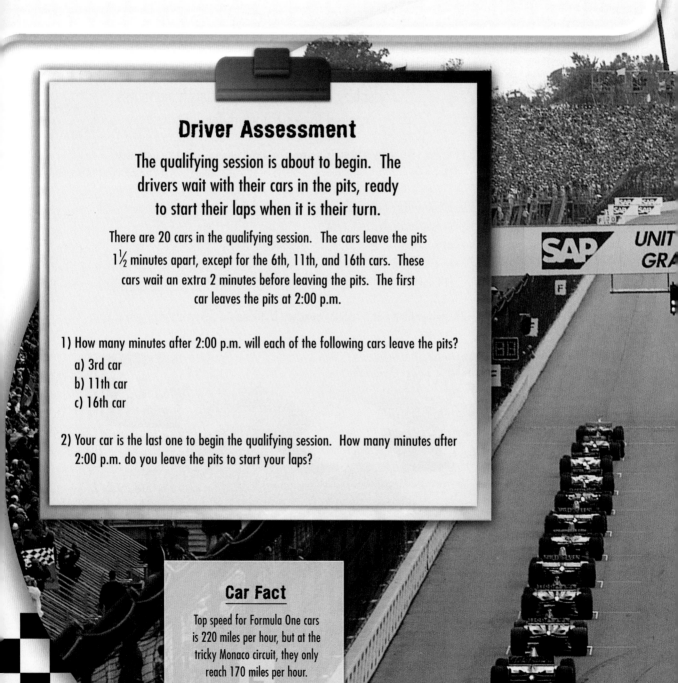

Driver Assessment

The qualifying session is about to begin. The drivers wait with their cars in the pits, ready to start their laps when it is their turn.

There are 20 cars in the qualifying session. The cars leave the pits $1\frac{1}{2}$ minutes apart, except for the 6th, 11th, and 16th cars. These cars wait an extra 2 minutes before leaving the pits. The first car leaves the pits at 2:00 p.m.

1) How many minutes after 2:00 p.m. will each of the following cars leave the pits?
   a) 3rd car
   b) 11th car
   c) 16th car

2) Your car is the last one to begin the qualifying session. How many minutes after 2:00 p.m. do you leave the pits to start your laps?

Car Fact

Top speed for Formula One cars is 220 miles per hour, but at the tricky Monaco circuit, they only reach 170 miles per hour.

Math Challenge

The qualifying session is over and the flying lap times have been used to determine the positions of all the cars on the grid.

Here are the top six flying lap times, including your own. Below, you will see the first six cars in formation on the grid. Can you figure out which car belongs in which position

BMW WilliamsF1 driver's time: 74.6 seconds

Ferrari driver's time: 75.1 seconds

Your time: 74.8 seconds

McLaren driver's time: 75.0 seconds

Renault driver's time: 74.9 seconds

BAR driver's time: 75.4 seconds

the grid at Indianapolis

6th

5th

4th

3rd

2nd

POLE POSITION

19

RACE DAY

It is the morning of the big race. Formula One cars have to start a race in the exact same condition as when they ended the qualifying session. The cars must have the same tires, and the teams are not allowed to add any extra fuel. During a race weekend, the cars are kept in a special area overnight. On the day of the race, the teams get their cars back at 8:00 a.m. There are a lot of final checks to be made before your car is due on the grid at 1:30 p.m. While your team works on the car, you must prepare for the race. You won't have much free time. You'll have to give TV interviews, attend the team briefing, and take part in the drivers' parade.

Driver Assessment

On the morning of a race, drivers are very busy.
Here are some activities the drivers will have to do:

- meet with engineers
- make final checks on car
- take part in drivers' parade
- put on helmet
- eat breakfast
- meet reporters

Here are the times for these activities:

- 1:50 p.m.
- 8:30 a.m.
- 11:30 a.m.
- 9:30 a.m.
- 12:00 p.m.
- 1:30 p.m.

Can you match the times and activities to the photographs?

C

D

A

B

20

Math Challenge

It is 10:20 a.m. Your team still has a number of repairs to make before the race. The team has 3 hours and 10 minutes left to complete the work.

Here is the amount of time needed for each repair. Will your car be ready when the race starts?

seat belt:	12 minutes
accelerator pedal:	58 minutes
rear suspension:	1 hour and 9 minutes
front bargeboard:	47 minutes

E

F

The Start of the Race

- 30 minutes to the start: cars leave the pits, take a lap around the track, and then line up in their grid positions.

- 15 minutes to the start: the pit exit is closed.

- 10 minutes to the start: all people must leave the grid except for the drivers, team technical staff, and officials.

- 5 minutes to the start: a series of lights at the grid now signals the countdown to the start of the race.

- 3 minutes to the start

- 1 minute to the start: engines are started.

- 15 seconds to the start

- Cars run a "formation lap" to warm up their tires, but stay in their grid positions.

- When all the cars are back on the grid, the final countdown begins.

- 5 seconds

- 4 seconds

- 3 seconds

- 2 seconds

- 1 second

- The race director will now choose when to start the race. When all the red lights go out, the race has started.

The Monaco Grand Prix has begun. Now anything can happen, from a mechanical failure to a dangerous crash. Whatever happens, it will probably happen quickly and at high speed! During a race, Formula One drivers need to concentrate hard and be ready to handle many different problems. The drivers also need to watch for different flags. These flags communicate messages to the drivers. Try a lap of the Monaco circuit, and see how well you handle hazards on the track and problems with your car.

Driver Assessment

The Monaco circuit is shown on these pages.

Driving through each section of the track takes 1 second, so a full lap will take 60 seconds.

Use a single die (from a pair of dice) to get an idea of how it feels to be in a race and suddenly be presented with unexpected problems.

• Write down a lap time of 60 seconds. Then, roll the die and start moving around the track.

• If you land on a section with a flag, check to see the message for that flag. Depending on the flag, you will either have to add seconds to your lap time or subtract seconds from you lap time.

How fast was your lap time? Try another lap. Did you beat your previous lap time?

END of race

No overtaking
ADD 5 seconds.

Pull aside, faster car overtaking.
ADD 3 seconds.

You have broken race rules. **You are OUT** of the race.

Oil or water on the track
ADD 10 seconds.

A hazard has been removed.
SUBTRACT 1 second.

You need to make a pit stop.
ADD 4 seconds.

Math Challenge

You are going 125 miles per hour (mph) and see an accident ahead. You need time to react, then time to brake.

Use the STOPPING DISTANCES chart (right) to answer the following questions.

1) If your car is 13 feet long, how many car lengths will it take you to stop if you are traveling at 40 miles per hour?

2) How many car lengths will it take you to stop if you are traveling at 70 miles per hour?

3) The figures for the reaction distances can be found in which multiplication table?

STOPPING DISTANCES

Speed (mph)	Reaction distance (feet)	Braking distance (feet)	Total stopping distance (feet)
20	20	20	40
30	30	46	76
40	40	77	117
50	50	125	175
60	60	180	240
70	70	242	312

TUNNEL

MAKING A PIT STOP

Your car's fuel tank is almost empty and the tires need to be changed. It is time to make a pit stop. The refueling equipment in Formula One supplies fuel to a car so fast, it could fill the tank of a normal passenger car in about 4 seconds! Your pit crew will only need 9 seconds to refuel the car, change four wheels, and check for any damage. The pit stop will add 29 seconds to your lap time, however, because you will have to slow down to drive in and out of the pits. The faster you can make your pit stop, the better. You are now in the pits, so sit back and let your expert crew do what it does best.

A Formula One car zooms into the pits.

Driver Assessment

Your pit crew consists of eighteen people. The crew members all perform certain tasks:

- Three people per wheel change the wheels.
- Two people operate the front and rear jacks.
- Two people operate the refueling equipment.
- One person guides you in and out of the pits with a "lollipop" (a round sign with a long handle that resembles a lollipop).
- One person cleans the visor of your helmet.

1) How many crew members change wheels?
2) In 20 teams of 18 people, how many people change wheels?
3) In 20 teams of 18 people, how many people refuel?
4) It takes 1 second to put 3 gallons of fuel into your car's fuel tank. You need to put in 27 gallons of fuel at your pit stop. Can your refueling be done in 9 seconds?

Math Challenge
READY, SET, GO!

A Formula One pit crew does its job in seconds. How quickly can you use your math skills?

You have 5 seconds to do each of these math challenges. Ask a friend to time you!

1) Recite the products of the 4 times (multiplication) table.
2) Starting with 2, add the first four even numbers.
3) State how many centimeters are in a kilometer.
4) Add 19, 20, and 21.

Race Fact

The only part of a Grand Prix circuit that has a speed limit is the pit lane. During a practice session, a driver can be fined a lot of money for going over the speed limit! When drivers enter the pit lane, they activate a speed limiter by pressing a button on the steering wheel.

0 SECONDS

Guided by the lollipop, a driver stops at the exact right spot in the pit lane. The pit crew members rush into position.

1 SECOND

Some crew members start undoing wheel nuts. Other crew members use jacks to raise the car off the ground. The refueler makes a connection. A crew member will also clean the driver's visor.

2 SECONDS

As some crew members remove the car's wheels, other crew members get the new wheels ready.

3 to 4 SECONDS

Crew members tighten up the wheel nuts. At each wheel, crew members raise a hand to indicate they are finished.

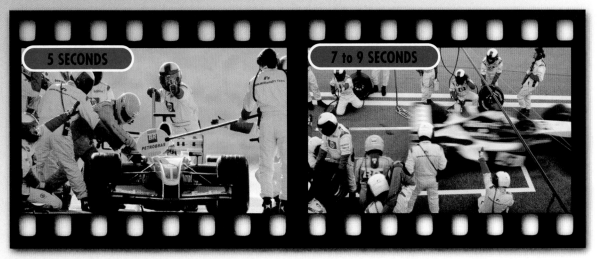

5 SECONDS

The car is lowered from its jacks. The lollipop tells the driver to select first gear and get ready to go.

7 to 9 SECONDS

The refueling is finished, and the crew removes the fuel hose. The lollipop is lifted and the driver shoots off.

Congratulations! You won the Monaco Grand Prix. You earned ten points, which is the maximum number of points possible for each race, and you stood on the winner's podium while your fans cheered. Since the Monaco Grand Prix, you have competed in many more races, and you finished in one of the first eight positions in every race. The Grand Prix season is nearing the end, however, and there are just three races left. The Drivers World Championship is won by the driver with the most points at the end of the season. If you are going to become world champion, you will need to drive very well in these last three races!

Driver Assessment

The results of the last three races will decide who wins the Drivers World Championship.

Use the DATA BOXES on page 27 to answer the questions below. The first box shows points awarded in a race. The second box shows points earned by the top six drivers (including you) before the last three races of the season. The third box shows points earned by the top six drivers in those last three races.

1) In what position did the BMW WilliamsF1 driver finish in the Chinese Grand Prix?
2) In what position did you finish in the Japanese Grand Prix?
3) The Renault driver ended the season with a total of 51 points. In what position did the driver finish in the Japanese Grand Prix?
4) Who has more points at the end of the season, the BAR driver or McLaren driver? What is the difference in points between them?
5) In what position must you finish in the Brazilian Grand Prix in order to win the Drivers World Championship?

Champion Fact

By the end of the 2003 season, Michael Schumacher had won a record six Drivers World Championships. He won in 1994, 1995, 2000, 2001, 2002, and 2003.

Champion Fact

At the 2003 Hungarian Grand Prix, Renault's Fernando Alonso became the youngest driver to win a race. Maybe he will be a champion in the future!

DATA BOX

Points for a race

POSITION AT FINISH	POINTS
1st	10
2nd	8
3rd	6
4th	5
5th	4
6th	3
7th	2
8th	1

DATA BOX

Total points earned before the last three races

DRIVER	POINTS
BMW WilliamsF1 Driver	73
YOU	70
BAR Driver	55
McLaren Driver	47
Ferrari Driver	68
Renault Driver	41

DATA BOX

Points earned in the last three races of the Grand Prix season

DRIVER	CHINA GP	JAPAN GP	BRAZIL GP
BMW WilliamsF1 Driver	4	10	6
YOU	8	6	??
BAR Driver	1	4	0
McLaren Driver	3	5	0
Ferrari Driver	10	8	4
Renault Driver	6	??	1

The checkered flag signals the end of the race.

It's time for the winners to celebrate!

Math Challenge

At the edge of the track, workers build the winner's podium!

They use nets (flat shapes that can be folded into solid shapes) to make boxes to stand on.

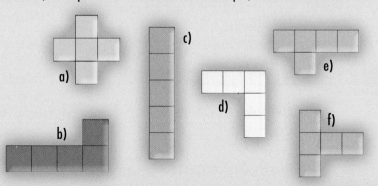

Which of these shapes are nets that can be folded to make a box with an open top?

PAGES 6-7

Driver Assessment

TOP TIP: To find the difference between two numbers, use subtraction. Subtract, or take away, the smaller number from the larger number to find the difference between the two numbers.

PAGES 8-9

Driver Assessment

A pictogram is a chart that uses an image to represent a set number of objects or actions. In the pictogram on page 8, an image of a complete car wheel represents taking 5 laps on a circuit.

The image can also be divided. This image represents two laps.

Math Challenge

When rounding numbers, always follow the same rules: if rounding to the nearest tenth, round up numbers that end in 5, 6, 7, 8, or 9 and round down numbers that end in 4, 3, 2, or 1. The number 36, for example, would be rounded up to 40, and the number 32 would be rounded down to 30. The lap lengths in the DATA BOX on page 9 are rounded to the nearest tenth.

When rounding decimal fractions to the nearest whole number, use the same rules. The decimal fraction 3.6, for example, would be rounded to 4, and 3.2 would be rounded to 3.

PAGES 10-11

Driver Assessment

TOP TIP: There are 60 seconds in 1 minute.

Math Challenge

TOP TIP: There are 60 minutes in 1 hour.

PAGES 12-13

Math Challenge

TOP TIP: Dividing by 100 is the same as dividing by 10 and by 10 again.

PAGES 14-15

Math Challenge

Angles are a measure of turn. Angles are measured in degrees. The symbol for degrees is °.

One whole turn (a complete revolution) measures 360°.

A quarter turn measures 90° and is a right angle:

There are four right angles in one whole turn.

The angles at the corners of squares and rectangles always measure 90°.

PAGES 16-17

Math Challenge

Perimeter is the boundary of a shape or area. The perimeter of a rectangle can be calculated in three different ways:

- Add all four sides.
- Add one long side and one short side and then double the answer.
- Double the length of the long side and the length of the short side and then add those numbers together.

The perimeter of this rectangle is 16 feet (ft).

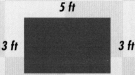

5 ft

3 ft   3 ft

5 ft

PAGES 18-19

Math Challenge

Numbers that put things in order, such as 1st, 2nd, 3rd, and 4th, are called ordinal numbers. Counting numbers, such as 1, 2, 3, 4, and so on, are called cardinal numbers.

PAGES 20-21

The Start of the Race

The patterns of lights shown on page 21 are used to communicate to the drivers before a race. In math, patterns can often be used to help solve problems. Always look for patterns in numbers and shapes. In the 5 times (multiplication) table, for example, the ending numbers of the products follow a pattern, alternating 0 and 5.

PAGES 24-25

Math Challenge

TOP TIP: 1 kilometer equals 1,000 meters, and 1 meter equals 100 centimeters.

When adding several small numbers, try to find pairs of numbers that make 10. In the Math Challenge, you are adding 2, 4, 6, and 8, so you can group together 4 and 6 in one pair and 2 and 8 in another pair. Each pair equals 10.

Multiplication can also make adding easier. Adding 19, 20, and 21 can be done quickly once you realize that adding these numbers is the same as multiplying 20 by 3. Just take 1 from 21 and add it to 19. Now you have three 20s!

PAGES 26-27

Math Challenge

Squares fitted together so that they touch on at least one side are called polyominoes. A polyomino made of five squares is called a pentomino. Below are 12 pentominoes. Of these pentominoes, 8 could be folded into a box with an open top.

ANSWERS

PAGES 6–7

Driver Assessment

1) The shortest distance is 199 miles to Monza in Italy. The longest distance is 10,193 miles to Melbourne in Australia.
2) 3,008 miles   3) 3,618 miles
4) 356 miles   5) 2,554 miles

Math Challenge

1) The month on the driver's calendar is July.
2) The driver is racing in Great Britain at the Silverstone circuit on the second Sunday (July 11).

PAGES 8–9

Driver Assessment

According to the pictogram, the number of laps for each Grand Prix is:

Australia	58 laps	United States	73 laps
Malaysia	56 laps	Great Britain	60 laps
San Marino	62 laps	Italy	53 laps
Europe	60 laps		

Math Challenge

1) Europe and Great Britain
2) Malaysia, Italy, China, and Japan

PAGES 10–11

Driver Assessment

1) Your times have improved by 15 seconds in cycling and by 21 seconds in running.
2) Your swimming time has become slower. You will need to improve your time by 6 seconds to match last season's time.

Math Challenge

1) You spent 9 hours, 35 minutes each week in the gym.
2) You spent 22 hours training each week.

PAGES 12–13

Driver Assessment

1) The car's width is about 6 feet.
2) The car's length is approximately 12 feet.
3) The car's weight with driver is at least 1,330 pounds.

Math Challenge

1) 24,000 hours of work for each person
2) 2,400 hours of work for each person
3) 800 hours of work for each person
4) 80 days

PAGES 14–15

Driver Assessment

1) The high downforce setting gives the fastest lap time

SETTINGS	LAP TIME (SECONDS)
LOW setting	75.3
MEDIUM setting	74.7
HIGH setting	**74.6**

2) The low gear setting gives the fastest lap time.

SETTINGS	LAP TIME (SECONDS)
LOW setting	**74.4**
MEDIUM setting	74.5
HIGH setting	74.8

Math Challenge

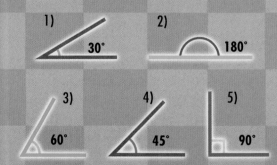

1) 30°   2) 180°   3) 60°   4) 45°   5) 90°

PAGES 16–17

Driver Assessment

1) At the start of the race, you will need 156 liters of fuel, or approximately 41 gallons.
2) You will need 104 liters of fuel at your first pit stop.
3) You will need 76 liters of fuel at the first and second pit stops and 84 liters of fuel at the third pit stop.

Math Challenge

1) The perimeter of the area is 22,610 feet.
2) The perimeter of the rectangle is about 6 inches.
3) The length of each side of the regular hexagon is 5 inches.

PAGES 18–19

Driver Assessment

1) The 3rd car leaves 3 minutes after 2:00 p.m.
2) The 11th cars leaves 19 minutes after 2:00 p.m.
3) The 16th car leaves $28\frac{1}{2}$ minutes after 2:00 p.m.
4) Your car leaves $34\frac{1}{2}$ minutes after 2:00 p.m.

Math Challenge

6th — BAR (75.4 seconds)
5th — Ferrari (75.1 seconds)
4th — McLaren (75.0 seconds)
3rd — Renault (74.9 seconds)
2nd — Your car (74.8 seconds)
POLE — BMW WilliamsF1 (74.6 seconds)

PAGES 20–21

Driver Assessment

Photo B: Eat breakfast (8:30 a.m.)
Photo E: Meeting with engineers (9:30 a.m.)
Photo F: Drivers' parade (11:30 a.m.)
Photo A: Meet reporters (12:00 p.m.)
Photo D: Put on helmet (1:30 p.m.)
Photo C: Make final checks on car (1:50 p.m.)

Math Challenge

The team will need 3 hours and 6 minutes for repairs. Your car will be ready in time.

PAGES 22–23

Math Challenge

1) 9 car lengths   2) 24 car lengths
3) 10 times (multiplication) table

PAGES 24–25

Driver Assessment

1) 12 crew members change wheels.
2) 240 people change wheels.
3) 40 people refuel.
4) Yes! In 9 seconds, you will have time to put in 27 gallons of fuel.

PAGES 26–27

Driver Assessment

1) The BMW WilliamsF1 driver finished 5th.
2) You finished 3rd in the Japanese Grand Prix.
3) The Renault driver finished 6th.
4) The BAR driver finishes with 5 more points.
5) You must finish 1st to win the championship.

Math Challenge

a, b, e, and f can be folded into boxes with open tops.

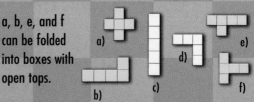

a) b) c) d) e) f)

GLOSSARY

BARGEBOARD: a piece of bodywork on each side of a Formula One car that helps air flow more smoothly past the car

CHASSIS: the main framework of a car, which connects to the engine, suspension, and body parts

COCKPIT: the interior of a vehicle, such as a race car or airplane, where the controls of the vehicle are located

CONSTRUCTORS: in Formula One, the teams of people who design, build, and race the cars

DOWNFORCE: a downward force created when air flows past the wings of a Formula One car, helping the car stick to the road

DRAG: the resistance air creates for something moving through it, such as a car or a plane

ENGINEERS: people who use math and science for practical tasks, such as designing and building structures or vehicles such as Formula One cars

FORMATION LAP: a lap around the track just before the start of a Grand Prix, with all the cars staying in grid formation

GEARBOX: also known as the transmission, the part of a car that holds different gears to allow the car to be driven at different speeds

HAIRPINS: extremely sharp bends on race tracks

HEXAGON: a two-dimensional (flat) shape that has six straight sides and six angles

JACK: a piece of equipment that is used to raise a car off the ground

LIFT: the upward force created when air flows past an airplane's wings

NET: a two-dimensional (flat) shape that can be folded to create a three-dimensional shape, such as a box

REGULAR: for two-dimensional (flat) shapes, having sides that are equal in length

ROLLBAR: a piece of equipment on a racing car that protects the driver if the car rolls over

SCRUTINEERS: Formula One officials who watch over the teams and their cars during a race weekend to make sure that no rules are broken

SPONSORS: in Formula One, companies that provide money to constructors in exchange for the constructors helping the companies advertise, usually by displaying a company's name on the cars and on a driver's clothing

STAMINA: the ability to keep going during a tough physical activity

STRATEGY: a plan of action to achieve a goal, such as winning a race

SUSPENSION: the parts of a car that attach the wheels to the car and help absorb bumps in the road

VISOR: the part of a Formula One driver's helmet that allows the driver to see out but still provides protection

Measurement Conversions

1 inch = 2.54 centimeters (cm)

1 foot = 0.3048 meter (m)

1 mile = 1.609 kilometers (km)

1 pound = 0.4536 kilogram (kg)

1 ton = 0.9074 metric ton (m ton)

1 gallon = 3.784 liters (l)